FOURTHQUARTER

HOW TO FINISH YOUR COURSE

WITH JOY

DON SISK

Striving Together Publications
4020 E. Lancaster Blvd.
Lancaster, CA 93535
800.201.7748

Edited by Cary Schmidt
Cover design by Andrew Hutchens
Layout by Beth Lee and Craig Parker

ISBN 978-1-59894-171-5
Printed in the United States of America

Dedication

I dedicate this book to my pastor,
Dr. Paul Chappell.

Dr. Chappell has always been a friend to older
preachers. He has listened to and honored men who
have been in the ministry for many years. I was nearing
my "Fourth Quarter" days when I met him some twenty
years ago. His encouragement and his friendship have
been a great blessing to me.

The opportunity to be a part of the ministry of
Lancaster Baptist Church and West Coast Baptist College
has helped to make my "Fourth Quarter" a very fruitful
and pleasant experience.

Acknowledgments

I am grateful for the many people who have assisted in the publication of this book.

I am especially grateful for Pastor Cary Schmidt for editing the book and for his encouragement to me during the writing. I thank the entire staff of Striving Together Publications for their help. I thank Beth Lee for her excellent layout efforts, and Andrew Hutchens for his effort in designing the cover.

I thank God for two great organizations, Baptist International Missions and Lancaster Baptist Church, for allowing me the privilege of ministering with them for these many years.

Most of all, I thank the Lord that He has allowed me to live long enough to write a book of this nature.

Table of Contents

Foreword

If there has ever been a man who knew how to make his "fourth quarter" count, it is Dr. Don Sisk. This man of God has been greatly used in the Lord's work through many years of his life, but especially in my life during his fourth quarter years.

I first met Dr. Sisk when he served as the Director/President of Baptist International Missions, Inc. That meeting was a milestone event in my life, although I didn't know it at the time. Over the years, Dr. Sisk has been a friend and mentor to me, providing help, encouragement, guidance, and counsel beyond what I can describe. He has had a tremendous influence on our church and has made a great investment into our West Coast Baptist College students.

When I think of Dr. Sisk freely giving of himself to me and to our ministry during the season of life when many would retire and relax, I am deeply grateful. To me, the value of having a man like Dr. Sisk involved in our ministry is similar to that of a seasoned player on a sports team who willingly helps the young players learn the game. Like a star athlete who simply loves the game, Dr. Sisk's joyful spirit is contagious. His influence has caused many people to love the Lord, to love ministry, and to serve God more effectively.

Dr. Sisk has been used of God in hundreds of churches and on mission fields around the world. He has given of himself to encourage, mentor, and advise countless missionaries and pastors. Only eternity will reveal the impact of this man's life and ministry—the millions of dollars given to missions, the missionaries on the fields, and the souls saved because of his influence.

I'm thankful Dr. Sisk has passionately served God during his fourth quarter and that he has written this book to encourage others to do the same.

Dr. Paul Chappell
Lancaster, California
June 2011

Introduction

Several years ago God began to deal with my heart about the great number of people who retired and soon after retirement, began to have various kinds of physical and/or emotional problems. Many of these had worked hard and had enjoyed good health for many years. Suddenly their lives took a tragic turn. In some situations they died soon after retirement.

The concept of a productive and purposeful life suddenly coming to a standstill simply because of "retirement" greatly bothered me. God has convicted me to make eternal use of every day that He has given me to live.

I was watching a football game one night several years ago. It was a bowl game. The coach had reached mandatory retirement age and this was his last game. His team won the game. The team hoisted the coach on their shoulders and carried him off the field. I saw the look in his eyes. It seemed to say, "I can still coach; I don't want to retire." He had been one of the most successful college football coaches of all time. Sadly, just a few months after his retirement, he passed away. When I heard of his death I thought, "Coaching football was his life. He had nothing left for which to live."

Another man, with whom I am familiar, had worked in coal mines for his entire adult life. He retired on a Friday. The following Thursday, less than a week after his retirement, he had a heart attack and slipped into eternity.

We could go on recounting story after story of great people who retired and immediately began to have physical problems. Within a short time of retirement, they became nearly inactive. Purpose and direction in life seemed to have a dramatic and perpetual pause.

God made us for a purpose. When we do not have a purpose for living, we begin to deteriorate. In reality, without a purpose, we cease to live.

When we see the definitions for *retire*, they don't look like a desired situation. Think about this word for a moment:

re·tire

—verb (used without object)

1. to withdraw, or go away or apart, to a place of privacy, shelter, or seclusion.
2. to go to bed:
3. to withdraw from office, business, or active life, usually because of age:
4. to fall back or retreat in an orderly fashion and according to plan, as from battle, an untenable position, danger, etc.
5. to withdraw or remove oneself.

—verb (used with object)

6. to withdraw from circulation by taking up and paying, as bonds, bills, etc.; redeem:
7. to withdraw or lead back (troops, ships, etc.), as from battle or danger; retreat:
8. to remove from active service or the usual field of activity, as an army officer or business executive:
9. to withdraw (a machine, ship, etc.) permanently from its normal service, usually for scrapping; take out of use.

—noun literary

10. a place of withdrawal; retreat:
11. retirement or withdrawal, as from worldly matters or the company of others.

Of all of these definitions, I found number nine to be the most revealing: "to withdraw permanently from normal service usually for scrapping; take out of normal use."

Who wants to withdraw permanently? Who wants to be scrapped? Who wants to be taken out of normal service? What an undesirable position in life!

The average life expectancy in America is now nearing eighty years. This has dramatically increased over the past seventy-five years. Most men and women can expect to live longer than previous generations in our country. And yet, it is not unusual to find people in their late fifties and early sixties entering retirement. In light of present life expectancy, this means that most retired men and women can expect to live another twenty years!

Your last twenty years, if God blesses you with them, are essentially your "fourth quarter." Your first twenty years, you prepared to live your adult life. Your middle forty years, you expended your life on whatever purpose and values you determined important. Perhaps now, you are approaching that last twenty years. Perhaps you are already in those last twenty—your own fourth quarter.

No winning team retires from the game after three quarters of play. If anything, a winning team desires for the fourth quarter to be their best performance. Though tired, a winning team stays engaged and focused during the fourth quarter.

What will you do with those twenty years? What will you do with your fourth quarter?

This is the question that we will examine in the following pages.

ONE

A Great Fourth Quarter

I n sports, the most important part of the game is how the last few minutes are played. In football, this would be the fourth quarter. In college basketball, this would be the last ten minutes. In pro basketball, again this would be the fourth quarter.

Can you imagine a team playing great for three quarters and then the coach deciding to take all of the starters or his best players out for the fourth quarter? Or imagine a player giving it his all for three quarters but then demanding to be taken out for the entire fourth quarter to do something other than play the game. Both of these situations are absurd. The coach probably wouldn't be coaching very long with that philosophy. The player would not maintain a position on the team if he exercised such an option.

The result of the game is decided in the fourth quarter. A team may be far ahead, but if they do not play well in the fourth quarter, they could easily lose the game. On the other hand, a team may be far behind but make a great comeback in the fourth quarter. Fourth quarters are game makers!

The following story is the account of the greatest comeback in the history of college basketball. Ironically it just happens to be a victory for the Kentucky Wildcats, my favorite sports team.

Kentucky played as poorly against LSU in the first half and early second half as they ever have against any team. They were down by 31 points, and making such elementary mistakes that one might almost have expected Rick Pitino to stop the game, concede, and leave. Instead, Kentucky staged the greatest collegiate comeback ever, from a huge deficit to win the game 99–95, a new NCAA record. Duke held the previous record, when it was down 56–27 at the half against Tulane on December 30, 1950, yet came back to win 74–72 (according to the 1994 NCAA Basketball book).

Nothing went right for the Cats early in the game. Nothing. They had lost their last four games in a row in Baton Rouge, and this game seemed to be following a similar script. Andre Riddick put Kentucky ahead 1–0 on a free throw (missing the other), but LSU quickly zipped ahead on a Ceasar basket (which didn't occur until two minutes into the game). The Cats had several shots blocked when they were tentative inside the paint, and some awful three-point shooting assisted the Tigers in going up 7–1 with 4.5 minutes gone in the first half.

Riddick made Kentucky's first field goal shortly thereafter, but a total absence of defense allowed LSU's Lenear Burns to score and put the Tigers up 9–3. Pitino was so frustrated with his team's poor offensive performance that he benched Prickett, Rhodes, and Riddick in favor of McCarty, Brassow, and Martinez, in a single mass substitution.

LSU exhibited phenomenal shooting over Kentucky's zone, especially from three-point distance and despite occasional tight coverage. The Tigers seemed so much in control that ESPN felt able to switch coverage to the conclusion of the Villanova-Connecticut game. They returned later with LSU leading by 22–15 with 8 minutes gone in the first half.

Ronnie Henderson was absolutely unstoppable from the three-point line, shooting six for seven, even when closely guarded. Gimel Martinez was Kentucky's sole scoring source inside, getting 10 points fairly quickly to keep UK in the game. Gimel had 12 points by halftime and scored only one in the second half. By the time LSU had reached a 32–23 lead only one of Kentucky's starters had scored. A short time later, another Henderson three-pointer put LSU up 37–25 with 3.5 minutes left in the half, and an identical shot led them to strengthen their lead at 43–25. At this point, Henderson hit another three-pointer to put the Tigers up 46–25 with 2.5 minutes left. Prickett finally got a basket underneath to halt UK's scoring drought, and Ford hit a three-pointer to make the score 46–30.

Play was rough. Wildcat players were pushed around with no calls made, until finally the refs had to warn a group under the LSU basket to stop shoving. Rodrick Rhodes then pushed a Tiger player in front of an official and was immediately called for a foul. LSU had a 48–32 lead at the half. Kentucky's starters had only scored 9 points, and the Wildcats suffered from 39% first half field goal shooting.

Pitino benched Prickett and Rhodes to start the second half, going with Brassow and McCarty. A Brandon drive and two Henderson free throws put the Tigers up 52–35. Ceasar got five quick points and LSU led 57–37. A Kentucky player was knocked to the floor hard on the next UK possession, but no call was made, yet Travis Ford grabbed Ceasar's arm as he was shooting, and was called for a deliberate foul. (It probably was, but then so was the uncalled foul against the Tigers.)

A Brandon three-pointer, several Kentucky turnovers, and a Ceasar basket and free throw brought the score to 64–37. Travis Ford was playing badly, and Pitino played Epps for a while. More baskets by Ceasar put Louisiana State up 68–37, their largest lead of the night. It seemed at this point that everything was working for the Tigers, and the wheels were falling off for the Cats. The Tigers went on an 18–0 run against the Cats to create this lead.

Kentucky could have folded their tents and gone home, but instead they tried almost nothing but three point shots and were able shave the lead a bit. LSU visibly relaxed, and thought they had the game in the bag. They became careless with passes and missed many free throw opportunities. Brassow, Delk, Ford, and McCarty combined to bring UK within 12, and after an exchange of baskets, Brassow hit two consecutive three-pointers to bring the Cats within ten. McCarty made an inside shot which cut the margin to 82–74, then Burns and Rhodes fouled out for their respective teams.

A layup by Ford and a basket by Titus led to an LSU margin of 87–78. Despite making more turnovers, UK chiseled away at the lead when LSU became even sloppier and their hot shooting (68% for field goals in the first half) deserted them. A Ford three-pointer brought the score to 88–82. Henderson made a three, then Ford made an uncharacteristic travel when he took a step and found no one to receive his pass. With just over two minutes remaining in the game, a pair of Brassow three-pointers brought Kentucky to within three points, 93–90.

Ceasar was then fouled on a drive and hit his free throws making the score 95–90.

With a minute and forty seconds remaining, Tony Delk hit a three-pointer which brought the score to 95–93. Rather than using up the clock, LSU then turned the ball over to give new life to the Cats. Kentucky then turned the ball back over, but the Tigers lost the ball yet again. UK missed a three-point shot, but Brassow was fouled by Rubchenko. Jeff missed both free throws, but Kentucky somehow got the ball after it was knocked out of bounds. McCarty hit a three-pointer from the corner (right in front of the Kentucky bench, which was yelling at him to shoot), and his goal put the Wildcats up by 96–95 with 19 seconds remaining. LSU called its last timeout with 11.5 seconds left in the game. They needed to set up a scoring play. Kentucky saw the offensive set of the Tigers and called its own last timeout.

LSU ended up getting off a poor shot, which Tony Delk rebounded with 4.4 seconds left, and he was immediately fouled. Tony missed his first free throw, but hit the second for a 97–95 lead. To bring the ball in, LSU threw a long pass down court, but the LSU player fell down and was called for traveling. Ford was fouled on the inbounds play, and hit both his free throws with 2.2 seconds left, and that was the game. The final score was 99–95 with Kentucky outscoring LSU 62–27 in the second half to win the game.

Kentucky hit twelve of twenty-three three-point shots in the second half, and LSU missed eleven of twelve free throws in the game's final twelve minutes.

The primary purpose of these chapters is to encourage people in the fourth quarter of life. I urge you not to quit during what could be the most effective and incredible years of your life. I challenge you to live your final years productively.

You may have had an excellent three quarters up to this point, but you could lose your momentum in this fourth quarter. You may have had a rough three quarters, but you can have a comeback with a great fourth quarter.

By no means am I opposed to someone taking leave from a position in which they have labored for many years. It's a wonderful thing if you have built a retirement fund. Thank the Lord. You may no longer be required to do many of the things you did not enjoy about your job. You now have a chance do things that you really desire to do.

This would be a good time to make a couple of lists. Why not make a list of the things that you did not enjoy—

you did them because you had to. Then make a list of things that you really would like to do. Then, I urge you to read 1 Corinthians 12, and Romans 12. May I suggest that you seriously consider spending the last quarter of your life helping others? You are a vital part of the body of Christ, and God has strategically and purposefully placed you in a position to bless others and to be used by the Lord.

Again I am not saying that those in Christian ministry should stay in the same position of ministry until they die. The priests in the Old Testament did not function as priests until they died, but they were mentors for and helpers of younger priests. Even so, there comes a time in our lives when we would do well to step aside and allow younger men to occupy the positions that we have occupied. However, when we leave those positions, we should not sit idly by and do nothing. We should continue to engage in the work of God and in serving others.

You are a vital part of the body of Christ.

If you are age sixty or beyond, you still have much to offer the work of God and local church ministry. If you are a young leader and you know someone who is age sixty or beyond, be sure to help them have a great fourth quarter. Help them utilize their gifts and abilities for God's glory. I am afraid that we have failed to utilize the great potential of people in their fourth quarter of life. I am saddened by the large number of formerly greatly used men of God who are not using their influence and their God-given gifts in the latter part of their lives.

Some years ago, I made an important decision. I chose to stay actively involved in ministry after my "retirement." In fact, I personally never used the word. I simply saw myself relinquishing some responsibilities that I might take on some others. I relinquished my position as President/Director of Baptist International Missions. This decision represented a huge transition in my "fourth quarter" of life, and it required me to make some difficult decisions about what to do next. That experience is what I want to share with you in the next chapter.

TWO
Don't Quit Serving God

I preached my first sermon on December 1, 1954. On Thanksgiving night, November 25, 1954, I made my call to preach known to my church. My pastor, Brother W.E. Jones said to me, "Don, since God has called you to preach, you can preach for us at prayer meeting next Wednesday." I had not thought about preaching that soon, but since my pastor said I was to do it, I immediately began to nervously make preparation for that first sermon. My text was Matthew 27:24–35. I have no idea what the sermon was, and I'm thankful that we did not record our sermons back in those days.

About one year later, December of 1955, I was called to pastor two churches part-time, in western Kentucky. In February of 1956, I was ordained.

GOD'S LEADING

Intentionally, for all the days of my ministry, I have stayed busy. But as I approached the age of seventy, I knew that I would face some important decisions about my future. I had constantly told the responsible people at BIMI that I would not serve as the president past the age of seventy. As I began to make plans for a transition, some suggested that since I was in good health and the ministry was going so well, I should continue in that position. My answer was always the same. "No one knows when he gets senile. His friends would not tell him, and if his enemies told him he would not believe them." In reality, I knew that God was leading in my decision.

For over thirty years I had preached more than forty mission conferences each year in addition to fulfilling my administrative responsibilities as the first Far Eastern Director and then as the President/Director. During my time as director, I visited more than forty different countries. I had no idea what awaited me after the transition. My plans were tentative at best. I assumed, since I would not be the director of BIMI, that my invitations to conferences would subside. I knew that I would not have the administrative responsibilities. I really did not know what to expect or how God would lead.

One thing was certain. I desired to remain active in the work of God—expending my life for the cause of Christ. I had no desire to sit idly by and do nothing. I would often joke that I did not want to play golf every day—three times a week would be plenty. To be very honest, I had planned to play a lot more golf than I presently play, but the joy of what I have seen God do in recent years far outweighs the golf that I have missed.

I was more than happy to relinquish my administrative responsibilities at BIMI. At the time of my resignation from the directorship, BIMI had over one thousand missionaries in over ninety different countries. We had approximately eight thousand supporting churches and an annual budget of more than thirty million dollars. The thought of being free from that pressure was not looked upon as a loss, but as a relief. I really did not realize how great the pressure was until I was out from under it for a few weeks. It was a blessing to realize how free I was to do things that I desired to do, but previously did not have time to do. I believe that my decision was exactly what the Lord intended for me.

THE TRANSITION

The transition took place in June. My wife, Virginia, and I also celebrated our fiftieth wedding anniversary at that time. In July, I traveled to Lancaster, California, where I was speaking in the annual Spiritual Leadership Conference. During the meeting, Dr. Paul Chappell and Dr. Mark Rasmussen invited me to teach missions at West Coast Baptist College. I had very seriously considered spending a lot of time in bringing pastors to the World Mission Center of BIMI for a few days to make them acquainted with the mission organization. Harrison Bay, the location of BIMI, is situated close to a water sports area and a beautiful championship golf course. My thoughts were to entertain the pastors and their wives and make them acquainted with the day by day operations of BIMI. I believed that the more pastors could see what we do for missionaries, the more apt they are to send their missionaries through our organization. It would also give them greater confidence in supporting missionaries who are affiliated with BIMI. (Now that I think of it, that plan still sounds good. Maybe that can be my next project!)

After talking with Dr. Chappell and Dr. Rasmussen, Virginia and I began to pray about the many things that such a move would entail. The one thought we agreed upon was that it would be good, both for us and our successors at BIMI, if we were away from the daily operations. California would certainly be far away.

After much prayer and much deliberation, we agreed to come for one semester and teach some missions courses. If we had been asked to make a long-term commitment, I am not sure that we could have done that. We came for the spring semester in 2003. We have now taught every spring semester for the last nine years. Teaching college courses takes a lot of preparation and is quite difficult, but we have rejoiced in the opportunity and in the fruit.

OPEN DOORS

The Lord has also allowed me to continue to preach in missions conferences, travel to foreign countries, and preach in Bible colleges and seminaries around the world. Last year, there were only six Sundays that I was not preaching in a church. As you might have noticed, this is not typical retirement. However, it has been very good for us.

One of my great desires after the transition was to be a help to young pastors and missionaries. God has opened up so many doors and opportunities to minister that I am not able to accept half of the invitations I have received. Many churches in the west and northwest have been opened up for BIMI missionaries, and many of the West Coast Baptist College graduates have chosen to be affiliated with BIMI. Literally tens of millions of dollars have been given through the churches where I have had the privilege of presenting faith promise giving. What God has done and allowed us to be a part of in recent years has been astounding. We are grateful beyond words.

Presently, I am experiencing good health. To the glory of God, in the fifty-six years that I have been preaching, I have only missed one meeting because of a health problem. I doubt that I would have been as productive if I had continued as the director of BIMI. Neither would I have enjoyed the portion of health that I have.

Don't view your fourth quarter as a time to sit out.

Had I become inactive after the transition, I would have missed much and would not be as healthy mentally and physically as I am today. Remaining active in the Lord's work and in stepping through open doors has made a great difference in our lives.

Looking back on these decisions, I know they were right. I'm glad we didn't quit serving the Lord at "retirement." I'm delighted with the opportunities and fruit God has given us in these fourth-quarter years. And my challenge to you is simply—don't quit. Don't view your fourth quarter as a time to sit out. Find something that you desire to do for the Lord and do it with gusto. Live your fourth quarter to the best of your ability.

Most who read this book will not be preachers and will not have the opportunities for ministry that I have had. I have some good suggestions for you in the chapters ahead. But perhaps you are a preacher or a servant of the Lord. In the next chapter I would like to encourage you to stay in the work of God for the rest of your life.

THREE

Focus on Finishing Well

Regardless of how we enter the fourth quarter of life, we must concentrate on finishing well. If you have enjoyed success in your first sixty years of life, you should never take the attitude that you have done your part. I resisted this kind of thinking as I entered my own fourth quarter.

I remember a lady in her early fifties saying to me, "Brother Don, I have taught in Sunday school and Vacation Bible School for many years. I am ready to let someone else do this. I feel like I have done my part." I remember my reply to her. (By the way some fifty years later my reply would probably be more tactful.) I said, "If you have done your part, who do you wish to officiate at your funeral? Where do you wish to be buried? If you have done your part, it is time for you to die." Even though I would be more tactful, I still believe that today. As long as we are living and breathing, God has a purpose for each of our lives. When we have "done our part," when we no longer have a purpose for living, we may still be breathing, but we are not living. We merely exist.

FINDING THE POTENTIAL OF THE FOURTH QUARTER

What can you do after you are sixty years old? You could develop a tasty recipe for fried chicken and start a fast-food business. Colonel Sanders did. You could paint a masterpiece. Grandma Moses did. You could begin to study Greek. Oliver Wendall Holmes did. In fact he began to study Greek when he was ninety-four years old. When asked why he would begin a study of such a difficult language he replied, "If I don't do it now, I may never do it." (By the way, if you do not begin now to do some of the things that you are able to do and really desire to do, you may never do them.) The writer of Ecclesiastes exhorts us, "Whatsoever thy hand findeth to do, do it with thy might; for there is no work, nor device, nor knowledge, nor wisdom, in the grave, whither thou goest" (Ecclesiastes 9:10).

As a young preacher, I was always encouraged to see preachers who had ministered effectively for many years spending the latter part of their lives in helping young preachers reach their potential in the ministry. They could have just retired. They could have spent their last years fishing, playing golf, and traveling. Many preachers I knew chose to make the most of their fourth quarter. In doing so, they made a great impact and finished well.

As long as we are living and breathing, God has a purpose for each of our lives.

I heard Dr. John R. Rice preach effectively when he was well past eighty years of age. I remember seeing Dr. B.R. Lakin having to hold on to the pulpit to stand, and lifting all of us into the very presence of God as he preached on Heaven. I can see the arthritic, crooked finger of Dr. Lee Roberson in his mid-nineties encouraging us to stay faithful in our efforts to win a lost soul to the Lord. God used these and many others for many years after their primary ministries had ended. They may have relinquished some positions or titles, but they were faithful to do what they could to the very end. They finished well. These men were way ahead of the game entering the fourth quarter, but they continued to play hard until the game was over.

Several years ago, while ministering in a church in Virginia, I noticed that the young pastor had three older gentlemen who served in various ministries. When I inquired as to why he would have these older gentlemen on staff, he told me a wonderful story. He explained that none of the men were paid staff members. All of them had retired from their regular occupations. Each of them had decided to serve in the church without pay. He stated that they worked thirty to forty hours each week in the ministry. They had regular duties just as did the full-time staff members. One of them was in charge of hospital visitation. Another worked in the maintenance department. The third was involved with outreach and was training other soulwinners. These were some of the most joyful men I have ever met. They were doing things that they had always wanted to do. They were finally free from doing things that they did not enjoy. However, rather than just exist after retirement, they decided to live for the Lord and to be productive. Of course, they also knew that when they desired to take an extended vacation or to visit their children and grandchildren they were free to do that. They had all retired from their companies with sufficient funds, but they were playing well in the fourth quarter.

In several of the churches where I have visited, the pastors have had the same wisdom to utilize the valuable experience and potential of the retired members of the congregation. It is sad when young pastors miss this and feel that older church members have little to contribute to the daily ministry of the church.

Many years ago, I went to the headquarters of New Tribes Missions in Sanford, Florida. I learned that a large percentage of the office and maintenance staff were retired people who had gone there to live and to give their service to the mission. They could have played golf or gone fishing every day, but they chose to contribute their time and spiritual gifts to the edifying of the body of Christ.

One of my pet peeves for many years was that most missions classes in our independent Baptist Bible schools were being taught by people who had no personal experience in missions. I have also noticed that when many missionaries return to America, they often do not become involved in active missions ministries. How I have often wished for these servants of God to locate near a Bible college or a missions agency and use their valuable experience in assisting others. This is why I feel the Lord led me to begin teaching missions in Bible college after relinquishing my position at BIMI.

When God miraculously provided the large plot of land for the World Mission Center of BIMI, I immediately began to think of ways that this could be used to encourage missionaries to locate on the BIMI property after active missionary service. To the glory of God, several have done that and are performing many services for the organization. They gather every morning for prayer. They work in various clerical positions. Some help in maintaining the property. They encourage missionaries who come to the center. They often represent BIMI in missions conferences and in special missions services in the hundreds of churches that support BIMI missionaries.

Your greatest ministry may be in the fourth quarter.

Several years ago Dr. Roy Thompson informed me of a widow who desired to give her service to the missions organization. When I talked with her she told me very plainly that she would not accept any compensation for her work. All she asked for was a place to live. For many years, Joan Moody has wonderfully managed the guest rooms at BIMI.

A few years ago a pastor went to be with the Lord. His widow was greatly involved in the ministry of the church and had a great burden for missions. This dear lady, Hazel Mitchell, also came to BIMI and is graciously serving in various capacities.

While in Taiwan, a missionary informed me of a ministry in the city of Taichung. The pastor had been educated at a strong Bible college in the States, and his education had been paid for by a widow who had a great heart for missions. She spent the last years of her life in

Taichung. I could not help but think that she had left an eternal impression on the people of that city, and had personally been responsible for the education of a young Chinese pastor and the establishing of a good church. What a wonderful fourth quarter she had. Her fourth quarter investment continues to live on.

Use Your Most Valuable Years

I pray that many people who are in the fourth quarter will read this book. As you read, you may be asking, "What could I do?" May I suggest that you talk to your pastor and let him know that you desire to use your time and talents in the Lord's work. He may know of some great opportunities. There are many ministries that need to be developed, but the church may not have the financial means to pay someone. You may be the one to develop a new ministry in your church or to assist in an existing ministry. Many missionaries would be greatly blessed to have a retired couple come and help in their church, camp, or Bible college. Your greatest ministry may be in the fourth quarter. Bible schools and missions organizations all over the world would be greatly blessed to have some additional help.

One of my good friends and golf partners, Leo Walther, was not saved until he was fifty-seven years old through the outreach of Lancaster Baptist Church. When I first began to be involved in the ministries at Lancaster, he often transported me to and from the airport in his Lincoln Town Car. One day he jokingly said to me, "Brother Sisk, when I retired a few years ago, I retired rather comfortably. It would have been a lot more comfortable if I had not joined Lancaster Baptist." In reality, he knows that the best thing that ever happened to him was when he trusted Jesus Christ as his Saviour. For many years, Brother Walther has managed the media center, producing CDs and DVDs of the preaching services. In addition to that, he serves as a campus host, investing every day into the Bible college students with his loving personality and compassionate heart. He probably works an average of forty hours every week in the ministry. He was way behind when he entered the fourth quarter, but he is catching up. He is a winner.

You are no different than Leo Walther or any of these other examples. Your fourth quarter represents additional opportunities to expend your life for your Creator! Seize this quarter, and determine that you will finish well!

FOUR
Remaining Faithful for Life

For many years I have been associated with COEBA—an acronym for "Conference on Evangelizing Black America." I was the first white preacher to preach at this conference. In the opening remarks of my first message, I told the conference attendees that I felt like Jackie Robinson. I had broken the color barrier.

I was assigned the topic of "Finishing Well." That was fifteen years ago. I believe they thought, at that time, that I was about finished with my ministry. And since that time, my study has led me to read and research extensively the subject of finishing well. I have watched many who started well, but for one reason or another did not finish well. I have often considered the words of the Apostle Paul, "But I keep under my body, and bring it into subjection: lest that by any means, when I have preached to others, I myself should be a castaway" (1 Corinthians 9:27).

Paul plainly stated in this verse that he desired to finish well. He did not want to do anything that would prevent him from being fully used of God. He did not want to be a castaway. A castaway is something that is no longer capable of performing its intended purpose. We cast away a pen that will not write. We cast away a worthless automobile as scrap in a junk yard. We cast away food that is expired. No one desires or plans to be a castaway; however, many become castaways.

The thoughts in this chapter and the next—how to stay faithful in ministry for your whole life—are primarily designed for full-time Christian ministers, but they apply to every Christian. After all, we are all ministers—"Let a man so account of us, as of the ministers of Christ, and stewards of the mysteries of God. Moreover it is required in stewards that a man be found faithful" (1 Corinthians 4:1–2). Every born again believer is a minister and a steward. Another good word for *minister* is the word *servant*. Our one stated requirement is that we be found faithful.

In 2 Timothy, the Apostle Paul stated that he had reached his goal of being faithful—not being a castaway.

Look at his victorious benediction as he faces his soon coming execution:

Second Timothy 4:6–8 says, "For I am now ready to be offered, and the time of my departure is at hand. I have fought a good fight, I have finished my course, I have kept the faith: Henceforth there is laid up for me a crown of righteousness, which the Lord, the righteous judge, shall give me at that day: and not to me only, but unto all them also that love his appearing."

In verse 6, he was not morbidly bemoaning the fact that he would soon become a martyr. He was triumphantly proclaiming that he was voluntarily offering himself to the Lord. Then he stated his confidence. He was not thinking that this was his end. He was looking at death as a journey. He stated "the time of my departure is at hand." In other words, I am leaving one place and going to another place. It is like a ship leaving dock for another port. It is like a man taking his tent from one place to another. Paul knew that he would soon depart.

Every born again believer is a minister and a steward.

He also knew where he was going. "We are confident, I say, and willing rather to be absent from the body, and to be present with the Lord" (2 Corinthians 5:8). He knew that the moment he drew his last breath, he would be in the presence of the Lord. Rather than dreading death, he looked forward to it. Philippians 1:23–24 says, "For I am in a strait betwixt two, having a desire to depart, and to be with Christ; which is far better: Nevertheless to abide in the flesh is more needful for you."

A LIFE OF PURPOSE

Paul testified that his sole purpose in living was that Christ might live through him—"For to me to live is Christ" (Philippians 1:21). Thus, rather than a morbid scene, this chapter is a victorious rendering of the homegoing of a great Christian warrior.

Verse 7 is much like the words that Jesus Christ uttered in John 19:30, "When Jesus therefore had received the vinegar, he said, It is finished: and he bowed his head, and gave up the ghost." The statement, "It is finished" is powerful. It is like an artist putting the final touch on a masterpiece, then stepping back, looking at it, and proclaiming, "It is finished!" It is similar to a hard-fought athletic event when the winner realizes that he is victorious. In this powerful statement, Jesus proclaimed that everything that needed to be done for lost humanity to be saved had been done. He had shed His blood. He had defeated Satan by living a perfect life. He had paid the price of redemption. He had finished the work that he came to accomplish. In John 4:34 we read, "Jesus saith unto them, my meat is to do the will of him that sent me, and to finish his work." Thank God He finished! Salvation is a finished work.

A LIFE OF FAITH

Paul stated three things that his imminent death would mean.

I have fought a good fight. As long as we are in the flesh we must fight. Life is a constant fight with the world, the flesh, and the devil.

I have finished my course. Paul finished well. I think he must have had a relay race in mind. He did not say, "I have finished the race." He said, "I have finished my course." He had finished his part of the race and was handing the baton to the next runner. By the way, his transfer of the baton was well done. He was handing it off to Timothy, and he told Timothy that he had the same responsibility to pass the baton to the next generation. Second Timothy 2:1–2 instructs, "Thou therefore, my son, be strong in the grace that is in Christ Jesus. And the things that thou hast heard of me among many witnesses, the same commit thou to faithful men, who shall be able to teach others also."

Paul was not satisfied simply to finish well, but was desirous that those who followed him would also finish well and transition well. I love the statement, "There is no success without a successor."

I have kept the faith. The faith is the body of truth that had been given to the Apostle Paul. In spite of many battles and many persecutions, he had been true to the revealed Word of God until death. What a glorious benediction to a victorious life. What a wonderful goal for a well-lived life.

Presently, the Lord has allowed me to serve Him for fifty-six years. I share the passion and desire of the Apostle Paul. I want to fight a good fight, finish my course, and keep the faith. I don't want to be a castaway. And perhaps more importantly, I want to help those coming behind me to finish their course as well.

Do you dream of finishing well? Do you desire to finish your fourth quarter in the service of the Lord Jesus Christ? In the next chapter I want to share some specific things that God has used to allow me to faithfully serve the Lord over five and a half decades.

FIVE

Get In to Stay In

S taying in the ministry for the rest of your life requires a determined effort to serve the Lord with your whole heart for the duration—it is a long-term proposition. The ministry is not a hundred-yard-dash; it is a marathon. If we entered the ministry with a "try it and see if it works out" mentality, then our ministry will end in failure. To serve God for your whole life, you must not have a plan B "in case things don't work out." Ministry is not something that will work out. One must work at it.

WHOLLY COMMIT

In 1 Kings 19:19–21 we read the calling of Elisha—"So he departed thence, and found Elisha the son of Shaphat, who was plowing with twelve yoke of oxen before him, and he with the twelfth: and Elijah passed by him, and cast his mantle upon him. And he left the oxen, and ran after Elijah, and said, Let me, I pray thee, kiss my father and my mother, and then I will follow thee. And he said unto him, Go back again: for what have I done to thee? And he returned back from him, and took a yoke of oxen, and slew them, and boiled their flesh with the instruments of the oxen, and gave unto the people, and they did eat. Then he arose, and went after Elijah, and ministered unto him."

After Elisha realized that God was calling him to minister to Elijah, he turned his back on the past and gave himself wholly to serving God. The oxen were his livelihood, and he slew them. He burned his plowing instruments for firewood to boil the oxen. He completely surrendered his other options and wholly committed himself to serving God.

If you are going to stay in the ministry all your life, you must "get in to stay in."

Simon and Andrew did the same thing in Mark 1:17–18, "And Jesus said unto them, Come ye after me, and I will make you to become fishers of men. And straightway they forsook their nets, and followed him." Notice the word *straightway*. It literally means "immediately." They immediately left their nets behind and began to follow the Lord. Their nets were their livelihood. This action indicated to everyone who knew them that fishing (for fish) was over, and for the rest of their lives they would fish for men. In the same chapter it is stated of James and John, "They left their father Zebedee in the ship with the hired servants and went after him."

If you are going to stay in the ministry all your life, you must "get in to stay in." There must be total, unreserved commitment to the task to which you have been called.

DETERMINE TO BE FAITHFUL ALL THE WAY

On Thanksgiving night, 1954, we held a special service in the Black Oak Baptist Church. For some time God had been dealing with me about the ministry. I can honestly say that I never ran from the ministry. In fact, I think I may have known from the time of my conversion that I would one day be a preacher. I can remember more than once, while walking back home from my girlfriend's house after church, actually practicing the sermon that the preacher had preached that night. Perhaps I was aspiring to the ministry before I even realized it—for Paul said in 1 Timothy 3:1, "…if a man desire the office of a bishop, he desireth a good work."

My hesitation was that I did not believe that anyone would ever want to listen to me preach. Dr. Adrian Rodgers used to say humorously, "Many people feel that they have been called to preach, but the only trouble is, God has not called anyone to listen to them!" I guess that's how I felt—no one would care to hear me.

About that time, several men in our church publicly committed themselves to be preachers. Every time someone would make such a commitment, I would breathe a sigh of relief and think, "Good. God now has all the preachers He needs." However that did not relieve me. I knew in my heart that God was calling me to preach. Thus, on that Thanksgiving night, I went forward at the invitation and said to a personal worker, "Brother Humble, I do not know how I can preach, but I know God is calling me."

I remember the question he asked me. He said, "Don, how did you get saved?" My reply was that I was saved by the grace of God. He then said, "If you preach, you will have to do it by the grace of God." That was good advice in 1954. It is good advice today! After fifty-six years of preaching, I realize that by the grace of God I am what I am. I am thankful that the grace of God has enabled me to preach the glorious Gospel of Jesus Christ to a lost and dying world for all these years.

I can well remember a statement that I made that night. As I gave the testimony of God's calling and my surrender, I said, "I am going to be a preacher, even if I have to just live on bread and water for all my life." I have often thought how ignorant I was in that statement. I should have known that God doesn't feed his preachers just bread and water. I was very sincere, but far from accurate in my understanding. My heart's intent was simply to surrender. Regardless of what I would go without or where God would take me, I desired to follow Him.

I was listening to the Katle Tabernacle Program one Sunday and heard Dr. Katle relate a story about a young man who surrendered to preach. He was telling God that he desired to be a preacher, even if it meant he had to eat nothing but bologna for the rest of his life. Dr. Katle then informed the young man that God did not own a bologna factory, but that He did own the cattle on a thousand hills and that he should pray for beef steak! I related that story in a sermon in Japan one time, and a young Japanese preacher began to pray for beef steak. God led me to provide that for him, but I was shocked to discover that the steak he desired was priced at more than fifty dollars. (Therefore, I deleted that illustration from any future sermons in Japan!)

Your service for the Lord is not in vain!

God's Word is filled with statements that encourage us to be faithful. Here are just two:

> *Therefore, my beloved brethren, be ye stedfast, unmoveable, always abounding in the work of the Lord, forasmuch as ye know that your labour is not in vain in the Lord.*—1 CORINTHIANS 15:58

> *And let us not be weary in well doing: for in due season we shall reap, if we faint not.*—GALATIANS 6:9

God, through His Word, is saying to us, "Don't quit. Be faithful. Your service for the Lord is not in vain!"

Solomon had everything that a man could possibly desire materially, and yet concluded, "All is vanity" (Ecclesiastes 12:8).

Paul suffered unbelievable persecutions and trials, and yet declared it was "not in vain" (1 Thessalonians 2:1).

God may not "pay off" at the end of each day, week, month, or year, but He is a faithful master, and He will most certainly reward your faithfulness! Therefore, if we are doing well, we should not be weary. We must keep on keeping on. Fifty-six years ago, at the Black Oak Baptist Church, I had a desire to stay in the ministry all my life. That is still my desire.

A few years ago, I was speaking at a conference in the Dallas area. The moderator of the meeting stood to introduce me and said, "Dr. Sisk has run his race...." When I stood to speak, I said, "I hope the moderator is not a prophet. If he is, I am dead." The truth is, as long as we are breathing, we are still running the race. "It ain't over till it's over"— not good English, but a great truth.

When it comes to ministry, be in it with your whole heart. Be in to stay in. Throughout your race, you will be tempted to quit. You will be disappointed many times. You will be treated unfairly. Remember who called you and what He has promised you.

One day Jeremiah decided to quit the ministry. "Then I said, I will not make mention of him, nor speak any more in his name" (Jeremiah 20:9). He was having a very rough time and decided he couldn't continue. How long did this last? I am not sure, but in the same verse we read these words, "But his word was in mine heart as a burning fire shut up in my bones, and I was weary with forbearing, and I could not stay."

The blessings of the ministry far outweigh the problems and the trials.

You got in, now stay in.

SIX

Rethinking for a Right Perspective

Finishing well requires a right perspective on some critical values. Many people don't do well in their fourth quarter because of some faulty understandings. In the next few pages I want to examine three thought patterns that are deadly for those who desire to finish their course with joy.

FAULTY PERSPECTIVE #1— THE MESSIAH COMPLEX

In 1 Corinthians 12, the Apostle Paul uses the analogy of the physical body to show the relationship of the various members of the church to one another. This is one of my favorite chapters in the Bible. It emphasizes the diversities and the unity of the body. The point that I wish to emphasize here is that no one can do everything nor does God expect them to do so. Only God is omnipotent. Only God is indispensable.

If we are not cautious, when in a position of leadership, we will develop what modern writers have identified as a "Messiah Complex"—the over-estimation of one's own importance. If you are going to stay in the ministry all of your life and be productive in His service, you must not develop a Messiah Complex. You must not begin to believe that you are indispensable. If you have already developed this complex, seek the help of the Holy Spirit in relinquishing such thinking.

God did not make us capable of doing or being everything.

God made us all unique. There are no two people in the world exactly the same. God loves variety. Abraham Lincoln is quoted as saying, "God must have loved common people because he made so many of us." In 1 Corinthians 12:18 we read, "But now hath God set the members every one of them in the body, as it hath pleased him." God designed me according to His will. The same is true for you and for the millions of others who are in the body of Christ. He did not make us capable of doing or being everything. You are not the Messiah.

This is a humbling thought, but God managed long before we arrived on the scene, and He will manage long after we are gone. In other words, He can function without us. You may be important to the church or to the organizations with which you are affiliated, but you are not indispensable.

Even though we cannot do *everything*, thank God each of us can do *something*. We all have at least one spiritual gift. God has a specific plan and an eternal purpose for each of us. Thus, rather than complaining about what I can't do, I should find my purpose in the body of Christ and fulfill that purpose with joy. Thankfully, I do not have to do everything. God does not require me to be anything more than He created me to be.

I often say that if I can get one good thought from a book, it was worth my time to read it. Recently while reading, I found this quote, "Every opportunity is not an obligation." That helped me. I do not have to respond to every invitation. I must guard my time to accomplish that for which God designed me.

My favorite book on leadership is Dr. J. Oswald Sanders book, *Spiritual Leadership*. I well remember the day that I read this statement: "God has given you all the time you need to do everything that He desires for you to do." I set down my book and thought, "I must be doing a lot of things that God does not desire for me to do."

Since I am not the Messiah, my time and my abilities are limited. Therefore I must not have guilt over things that I cannot do and things that I cannot control.

FAULTY PERSPECTIVE #2—
TAKING LIFE TOO SERIOUSLY

Finishing your course requires a sense of humor. We should all learn to laugh. The Bible has much to say about this. Proverbs 15:13 states, "A merry heart maketh a cheerful countenance: but by sorrow of the heart the spirit is broken." Proverbs 15:15 teaches, "All the days of the afflicted are evil: but he that is of a merry heart hath a continual feast." Proverbs 17:22 says, "A merry heart doeth good like a medicine: but a broken spirit drieth the bones."

Learn to laugh. Learn to develop a joyful spirit regardless of your circumstances. And, if you have a joyful heart, it would not hurt to let your face know about it. I smile a lot. I often am questioned as to why I smile so much. I usually respond by saying that long ago I learned that it takes twice as many muscles to frown as it does to smile, and I am just lazy.

It is good to laugh at yourself. When others laugh at you, rather than getting angry, it might be good to laugh with them. When we were learning the Japanese language, our teacher often urged us to use what we were learning in class as we talked with the Japanese people. Of course we made many mistakes, and they would laugh at us. I usually laughed with them because I realized what a mess I had made with a language of which they are very proud.

I believe Jesus had a sense of humor. I think the disciples must have laughed when he said, "Ye blind guides, which strain at a gnat and swallow a camel" (Matthew 23:24). That may have provoked a big belly laugh from the disciples as they pictured a person getting all "out of sorts" about swallowing a tiny gnat and then swallowing an entire camel. If Jesus had desired to get His point across without humor He could have said, "You get very upset about small things, but allow giant errors without doing anything about them."

At another time He said, "Or how wilt thou say to thy brother, Let me pull out the mote out of thine eye, and, behold, a beam is in thine own eye?" (Matthew 7:4). I can hear Peter or John laugh out loud when they visualize a man with a large two-by-four in his eye trying to remove a speck out another's eye. Again, if Jesus had only desired to get the point across, He could have said, "You are quick to criticize others for small infractions, but you have great character flaws that are obvious to others."

A well-timed funny story can relieve tension. An appropriate joke, well told, can turn a potential controversial conversation into a sane discussion. Laughter is good medicine. Get a big bottle of it, and use it often. There are no side effects.

Faulty Perspective #3—Covering Rather Than Admitting Mistakes

Proverbs 28:13 says, "He that covereth his sins shall not prosper: but whoso confesseth and forsaketh them shall have mercy." When you blow it, admit it and seek forgiveness. We often think that if we admit to being wrong, we will lose the respect of others. But the opposite is true. People appreciate transparency and authenticity.

If I say to a class that I am teaching, "Yesterday I made a statement concerning a subject. After returning to my office I realized that I was wrong." Would that cause them to think less of me? Would that cause them to lose respect for me? No. My students know that I am not infallible. Admitting to my mistake would only increase their respect for me. If you are a pastor, your flock knows that you are not infallible. Therefore when you blow it, just admit it. Husband, your wife and children also know that you make mistakes. When you blow it, admit to them that you blew it and make it right.

I shall never forget punishing my son hastily for an incident. I later learned that he was innocent. It was difficult, but I said to Tim, "Forgive me. I should not have punished you for that. I was wrong." He didn't say it, but he probably thought, "That doesn't lessen the pain I felt!" Seeking his forgiveness actually helped our relationship.

Husbands and wives should be quick to admit when they blow it. Just admitting a mistake and asking forgiveness can prevent a lot of resentment. Ephesians 4:26–27 says, "Be ye angry, and sin not: let not the sun go down upon your wrath: Neither give place to the devil." Don't go to bed with unresolved issues. Don't let the devil get an advantage. It is difficult to say to your mate, "I blew it, I made a horrible blunder, please forgive me." However, those simple words actually build rather than destroy respect. You are not perfect, and it will not surprise anyone when you admit that you were wrong.

A strong fourth quarter requires that you sometimes rethink your game plan. Have you developed a Messiah Complex—attempting to do things God didn't design you to do? Are you willing to transition that thinking and adjust your life to God's game plan for your fourth quarter?

How about your sense of humor? Are you willing to laugh at yourself, and with others when they laugh at you? Let's face it, there are a lot of things about growing old that are actually very funny, especially to younger people. Be sure to enjoy the laughter.

And finally, how are you handling your mistakes? Those coming behind you would benefit immensely if you were willing to admit to those mistakes. Perhaps you could help others avoid them.

Be willing to move forward with a right perspective in these areas!

SEVEN

Come Apart

You have probably heard it all your life—"If you don't come apart, you will come apart." It is an old cliché. But more than a cliché, it is a biblical truth.

The disciples had been on a very successful missions trip. They had been sent by the Lord with specific instructions as to where they were to go and what they were to do. They had not only been commanded, they had been empowered by Him. In summing up their journey, we find these words in Mark 6:12–13, "And they went out, and preached that men should repent. And they cast out many devils, and anointed with oil many that were sick, and healed them."

They had done exactly what Jesus had commanded. They had experienced great victories. They were a happy bunch of evangelists. They had been very busy. (That is a common statement, is it not?) In fact they had been busier than most of us have ever been. Notice Mark 6:31, "And he said unto them, Come ye yourselves apart into a desert place, and rest a while: for there were many coming and going, and they had no leisure so much as to eat." Notice that last statement. They were so busy that they did not have time to eat. Most of us never get so busy that we do not have time to eat.

Success did not negate their need for rest— it made that need greater.

Their success did not negate their need for rest—it made that need greater. Great victories lead to exhaustion and fatigue. And fatigue makes us even more susceptible to temptations and periods of despondency. It is common for Christians to immediately enter a time of discouragement after a season of great victory—often due to exhaustion and depletion both physically and emotionally.

After Jesus performed the miracle of the feeding of the five thousand, He withdrew for a time of solitude with His Father. Elijah's request to die was soon after his great victory on Mount Carmel. And in this passage, Jesus encouraged His disciples to come apart and rest after they experienced a time of busy service.

For some reason, many have come to believe that the busier we are the more godly we are. In gatherings of Christians, it often seems like there's an unspoken contest to see who has been the busiest. (Just a tip—the one who first tells how busy he or she is always loses. The ones following will "out-busy" them every time!)

Unrushed Solitude

Actually there is no real value in being busy. Sometimes the most spiritual thing we can do is to be alone. Time alone with God is never wasted time. In fact it is the most profitable time that you will ever have. I think of great men such as Moses and Paul who had extremely long periods of solitude. It was during these times that they were strengthened for the great tasks that God had in store for them. The person who spends time before God will be well prepared to stand before men. He will be prepared to minister properly to men.

Every day we need to "come apart"—to find quiet, unrushed solitude with God. This involves time in the Bible and time to allow God to speak to our hearts.

Can you imagine anyone responding to an invitation from the President of the United States in this manner: "I am sorry, Mr. President, I don't have time to come to the

White House"? Can you imagine an aspiring basketball player who had received an invitation to practice with Michael Jordan responding like this, "Thanks, Mike, but I just don't have time to play ball with you"? Again, can

Time alone with God is never wasted time.

you imagine a young businessman saying to Bill Gates, "Thanks for the invitation, but I am too busy to sit in on your board meeting"? You would say that all of these examples are absurd. No one would do that. Yet every day millions of people who call themselves Christians neglect to spend time with the sovereign God of the universe. Their lame excuse is usually, "I didn't have time." Sure we have time. We must come apart and be still in the presence of God.

Every day we must come apart for a time of prayer—praising Him, making intercession for others, and confessing our sins and mistakes to Him. Prayer is asking and receiving. It is not just a spiritual exercise. It is an intelligent being conversing with another Intelligent Being.

I have often marveled at how specific the prayer of Eliezer was as he stood by the well expecting to find a bride for Isaac. Genesis 24:12–14 records, "And he said, O LORD God of my master Abraham, I pray thee, send me good speed this day, and shew kindness unto my master Abraham. Behold, I stand here by the well of water; and the daughters of the men of the city come out to draw water: And let it come to pass, that the damsel to whom I shall say, Let down thy pitcher, I pray thee, that I may drink; and she shall say, Drink, and I will give thy camels drink also: let the same be she that thou hast appointed for thy servant Isaac; and thereby shall I know that thou hast shewed kindness unto my master."

Eliezer was specific. Therefore, when God brought those things to pass, he knew that God had answered his prayer. Our prayers should not be comprised of purposeless or rambling words, but of specific and meaningful requests.

During our time in Providence, Kentucky, I read in the *Evansville Courier* a thrilling story about Dr. Earnest Reveal after his death. Dr. Reveal, who ran a rescue mission in Evansville, was known for his praying. The story related an incident when Dr. Reveal was resting by leaning on a column in front of the First National Bank. The president of the bank arrived, and upon seeing him with his eyes closed and leaning on the column, rushed in and said to one of the tellers, "Go and find out what Dr. Reveal is praying for and give it to him. If we do not, God may give him the entire bank!"

Just as our praying should be with purpose, so should our Bible reading. It should be systematic and consistent.

For over fifty years, I have read through the Bible at least one time every year. But I have learned it is helpful to vary my reading and, I have used various methods. I learned much when I began to read the Japanese Bible. A few years ago, while visiting in the church my son pastors, I was encouraged to read the entire Bible in ninety days. This was an incredible experience. That year I read the entire Bible four times. This year I am reading much slower and more devotionally. Vary your Bible reading, but by all means read God's Word.

I often hear people expressing a desire for more faith. I always instruct them, "If you desire to have more faith, read the Bible." The Bible says, "Faith cometh by hearing, and hearing by the word of God" (Romans 10:17). There are 7,487 promises in the Bible. By reading the Bible in one year, you will find an average of twenty promises every day. That will increase your faith!

EXTENDED SOLITUDE

In addition to our daily time with God, it is good for all of us to have extended times of solitude when we are not preparing sermons, working on business deals, or doing any other "work." These should be times to slow down and just soak up the joy of being in the presence of our great God. Not often do we take time to be holy. This may well be the reason that so many fall apart emotionally, spiritually, and morally.

A man once said to me, "I haven't had a vacation in ten years." I am sure that he wanted to impress me. I replied to him, "I am not a priest, don't confess your sins to me." Rest, relaxation, and recreation are not sinful, they are vital! Genesis 2:2 says, "And on the seventh day God ended his work which he had made; and he rested on the seventh day from all his work which he had made."

I can imagine someone asking, "Did God get tired?" I don't think so. Why does it say He rested? I really don't know. But I know He rested. If the sovereign God of the universe rested and the universe continued to function, perhaps the world would continue to function if you rested one day a week. (By the way, for any preachers and preachers' wives reading this, I hope you realize that Sunday is not your day of rest.)

Rest, relaxation, and recreation are not sinful, they are vital!

All of us need some time when we come apart from our regular routine. I suggest you have some hobby or activity that is quite different from your regular routine. For instance, if you are a mechanic, working on the family vehicles on your day off would not be a diversion from your regular work. If you are a preacher, reading and studying for sermons on your day off would not be a diversion. Those doing manual labor should probably do something that does not demand a lot of physical activity. On the other hand, those involved in office work or church ministries would do well to get involved in something that demands physical activity.

When I began to travel from church to church preaching in missions conferences and in Bible colleges, I was often with preachers who played golf. At that time, I had only played golf a few times. I was rather embarrassed when I went with men who were good golfers. I decided if I was going to be playing more often, I should buy my own clubs and take some lessons. The more I played the more I wanted to play. Golf became a good outlet for me. When I was playing golf I was free from the day-to-day problems. Thus the pressure was relieved. I functioned much better after exercising in that way.

To this day, I enjoy golf. It provides a time of fellowship with other men. Most golf courses have beautiful scenery, and time on a golf course diverts my mind from other things. I have friends who love gardening and yard work. I have one friend who loves to work on John Deere tractors. I often say that if he only had a half-acre of land, he would still buy a John Deere tractor just to have one to work with.

One day I was with a preacher friend who had invited me to preach. While in town, I was staying at his home as well. Early in the week, we drove past a golf course. He had no idea that I played golf, and he proceeded to explain how dumb he thought the sport was. He explained in detail how dumb it was to hit a ball and then chase it and hit it again.

On Friday morning, he ask me if I would like to go coon hunting. I explained that I did not have proper clothing for coon hunting, but he made plans for us to go. He lined up jackets, boots, and other equipment, and that night I found myself tromping through the woods with this man, listening to his dogs chase down tree raccoons. On top of not being a coon hunter, not being asleep, and not being able to golf that week, it was freezing. In the middle of it all, I began to consider—no one eats raccoons, and I couldn't see any other legitimate value to them, but these men greatly enjoyed the coon hunt.

When I finally got in bed around 2:00 AM, all I could think was, "You know, golf is not so dumb after all!" At one time in my life I liked fishing. I now often jokingly say, "If I had time and money, I would not waste them on hunting or fishing. I would do something constructive like playing golf." In reality I try not to be critical of what others enjoy. I just like to see people have something that will divert them from their regular work for a period of time. I am well aware that some people spend far too much time and resources on recreation—to the neglect of their work and calling for God. We must balance these things.

The bottom line is that we all need some rest. We all need to find a way to relax. We all need some kind of recreation to relieve our minds of the constant pressure of our day-by-day activities. Take a walk. Climb a mountain. Go to a ski resort. Lie in the sun and read a good book. God does not get angry when His children relax.

Parents, have you ever noticed how much pleasure you have when you see your children doing something that they really enjoy? Even so, you have a Heavenly Father who loves you, and He is pleased when you are enjoying His good gifts with your leisure time.

EIGHT

It's All about Him

Life and ministry are not all about us. They are all about Him. If the ministry is about us, we will ultimately be very frustrated and often defeated. Psalm 96:3 says, "Declare his glory among the heathen, his wonders among all people." First Corinthians 10:31 reminds us, "Whether therefore ye eat, or drink, or whatsoever ye do, do all to the glory of God." If we are anxious to declare His glory and to defer all the glory to Him, the things I will suggest in this chapter will not be difficult.

To finish well, we must learn to deflect the focus from ourselves and place it upon the Lord and others. Consider three principles that will help you keep your life and ministry "all about Him"!

LEARN TO REJOICE IN THE BLESSINGS AND SUCCESS OF OTHERS

Years ago, I took several seminary courses from a renowned Bible teacher. One of his favorite sayings was. "I don't understand it, but God often blesses people who disagree with me."

Would it not be a great lesson if we could understand that we are not in competition with other Christians? If we personalize this truth, rather than wondering why God gave some other person or some other ministry more than He has given us, we would rejoice with them. It really doesn't make any difference how much God blesses someone else—He will never run out of blessings. His blessings in the life and ministry of another in no way diminish His ability to bless me or my ministry in any way He desires.

I believe that we are immortal until God is finished with us here on earth. And when He is finished, it will be a good thing for us to leave this earth.

The Apostle John lived longer than any of the other apostles. All of the other apostles were martyrs, but God's plan for John was different. God had other things for him to do—such as write the book of the Revelation. John heard from some itinerant evangelist missionaries about a man by the name of Gaius. When John heard their good report, he was reminded of the time when he was used of God to bring Gaius to faith in Jesus Christ. When he heard about Gaius, he wrote in 3 John 4, "I have no greater joy than to hear that my children walk in truth." John rejoiced in the success of others.

God will never run out of blessings.

I have a sermon entitled, "What Makes an Old Man Happy." The idea for this sermon entered my heart one day when I was having lunch with Dr. Lee Roberson. As we fellowshipped, a man approached the table where we were seated and apologized for disturbing us. He then told Dr. Roberson about a Sunday twenty-five years prior. He had ridden a bus to Highland Park Baptist Church, and after hearing Dr. Roberson preach, he had trusted Jesus as his personal Saviour. I watched as big tears welled up in the eyes of Dr. Roberson. This great man of God was well into his nineties at the time, and he had accomplished much in his ministry. Yet nothing brought more joy to him than hearing about the success of those he had led to the Lord.

On one occasion in his latter years, Dr. Roberson was given a new Lincoln Town Car. On the Wednesday night after he had received the car, the long time associate pastor of Highland Park, Dr. J.R. Faulkner told me about the gift that Dr. Roberson had received. As he shared the news with me, I believe that Dr. Faulkner was more pleased that Dr. Roberson had been given the car than he would have been if the car had been given to him! This dear, selfless brother had learned to rejoice when God blessed other people.

There are a lot of burdensome things about growing old, but every one of them is greatly overshadowed by the news that I have been able to help or encourage someone else. Nearly every day, God allows me to cherish the news that God is blessing someone I know and love in the ministry. When I hear about their blessings, I am blessed.

Learn to rejoice when God chooses to bless someone you know and love.

DON'T ASSUME THAT ANYONE OWES YOU ANYTHING

Do you remember the story in Matthew 20 of the vineyard owner who hired laborers for his vineyard? The first men who went out early in the morning negotiated with him to work for a penny a day—a fair day's wage at the time.

None of the other laborers negotiated their wages. All they had was the word of the owner, "Whatsoever is right I will give you." Laborers were hired at 6 AM, 9 AM, noon, 3 PM and 5 PM. At the end of the workday, the laborers came to receive their pay. When the men who had only worked one hour received a full day's wage, the men who worked all day began to expect more. Yet, the vineyard owner gave them also a penny. Look at their response in Matthew 20:10, "But when the first came, they supposed that they should have received more; and they likewise received every man a penny. And when they had received it, they murmured against the goodman of the house."

The more you expect, the more disappointed you will be.

They had agreed to work for a penny a day. Look at the statement, "...they supposed that they should have received more." Their expectations changed when they saw the pay scale of others. We live in a similar generation. Most of the people of our country assume or suppose that people owe them something.

The simple truth is, the more you expect, the more disappointed you will be. Don't assume that just because you do something people owe you respect, compensation, or recognition. Many people quit the ministry because they were not treated in a manner they expected or assumed they would be treated.

You may say, "Brother Sisk, I am a charter member of the church, I deserve special treatment." "I have been in the ministry for fifty years" or "I am the senior pastor or have some other prominent position—people owe me something." May I suggest—the ministry is a privilege whether or not we are recognized, honored, or properly compensated!

Don't allow yourself to believe that anyone owes you anything. Rather than thinking about what you are going to receive, why not think about what you can contribute? Our God is a great paymaster. He will properly reward every one of His children. He does not pay at the end of the day or at the end of the week or month. But in time, and in eternity, He is always faithful to reward those who are faithful to Him.

CHOOSE TO BE THANKFUL

In Luke 17:12–29 we read the story of the healing of ten lepers. I can only imagine what each of them did when they realized that they had been healed. Perhaps one returned home to his wife and children and rejoiced with them about his healing. Maybe another returned to the office and told of his healing to his co-workers. I can see a young man returning to his friends and showing his leprosy free hands and face.

The amazing thing about this story is that only one turned back and gave thanks to the Lord. Luke 17:15–16 records, "And one of them, when he saw that he was healed, turned back, and with a loud voice glorified God, And fell down on his face at his feet, giving him thanks: and he was a Samaritan." We would think that the first thing that each of them would do is give thanks. Yet only one did.

We should keep the words "thank you" on our lips at all times. By the way, don't just keep them there to communicate to people who help you in some way. Many times each day, we should look heavenward and thank our great God for all that He is doing for us. We should look around us and express our thanks for those with whom we are associated. It costs nothing to express thanks, but it shows much.

It cost nothing to express thanks, but it shows much.

Jesus must have been pleased when this one Samaritan turned back to give thanks for what He had done for him. He is pleased when we thank Him and when, by word or written note, we express our thanks to others.

If you desire to finish well, if you desire to stay in the ministry all your life, these three principles are vital to remember and practice. Rejoice when others are blessed. Expect nothing. And constantly express thanks to God and others.

Remember, life and ministry are not all about "me." They truly are all about Him!

NINE
God Made You

The "fourth quarter" of any athletic event is so important. I recently watched the last few holes of the 2011 Masters Golf Tournament in Augusta, Georgia. At the beginning of the final round, a young twenty-one-year-old Irishman by the name of Rory McIlroy had a four stroke lead. He led for sixty-three of the seventy-two holes in the tournament. However, on the back nine, he fell to seven strokes over par. By the end of the tournament, he tied for fifteenth place and won $128,000, far less than he could have won. (Most of us wouldn't feel too bad about earning that much money for only four days of playing golf.)

On the other hand, Charl Schwartzel, a South African, was four strokes behind as he began play on the final day. He set a record by making birdie on the final four holes. He won the Masters and was presented with the coveted Green Jacket. His prize for winning was $1,444,000. He finished well.

In speaking of athletic events, the Apostle Paul wrote in 1 Corinthians 9:25–27, "And every man that striveth for the mastery is temperate in all things. Now they do it to obtain a corruptible crown; but we an incorruptible. I therefore so run, not as uncertainly; so fight I, not as one that beateth the air: But I keep under my body, and bring it into subjection: lest that by any means, when I have preached to others, I myself should be a castaway."

It is always too early to quit.

Charl Schwartzel spent countless hours practicing his golf game. He sacrificed and went without things that other young men enjoyed—all to be a great golfer. As a result, he received a huge reward. However, it is temporal. It will pass away.

The reward that faithful believers receive will be incorruptible. First Peter 1:3–4 promises, "Blessed be the God and Father of our Lord Jesus Christ, which according to his abundant mercy hath begotten us again unto a lively hope by the resurrection of Jesus Christ from the dead, To an inheritance incorruptible, and undefiled, and that fadeth not away, reserved in heaven for you."

Thank God we have a wonderful reward and future in Heaven!

I love the song that says, "It will be worth it all when we see Jesus." I am confident that any sacrifice we have made will seem very insignificant when we finally look into His eyes. Therefore, I urge you to keep on keeping on. Don't quit. It is always too early to quit.

Let me share a few more principles that have helped me to stay in the ministry. And yes, you have a ministry— all your life!

In 1 Corinthians 12, Paul uses the physical body as an analogy of the church. Notice what he says in verse 18, "But now hath God set the members every one of them in the body, as it hath pleased him." God made you. He made you what He desired for you to be. In chapter 4 he tells us that God has given us what He desires for us to have: "For who maketh thee to differ from another? and what hast thou that thou didst not receive? now if thou didst receive it, why dost thou glory, as if thou hadst not received it?" (1 Corinthians 4:7).

Paul asks two rhetorical questions in this verse. "Who makes you different from others?" The obvious answer is God. Again he asks, "What do you have that you did not receive?" Again the answer is obvious. Everything we have is a gift from God. We have no reason to boast. We have no reason to be jealous. We have no reason to complain. God made each of us. He gave each of us what He desired for us to have. Since this is true, we should have no problem with the following suggestions.

Be Content

Philippians 4:11 says, "Not that I speak in respect of want: for I have learned, in whatsoever state I am, therewith to be content." If I am to stay joyfully in the ministry all of my life, I must learn to be content. Paul said, "I have learned." Most of us would probably say, "I am learning." Hopefully we are growing in this area.

We should be content where God places us. I have lived in many different places. People often ask where I most enjoyed living. I honestly say, "I just like to live!" I have enjoyed every place God has allowed me to live. Wherever God places us, He has a purpose for us in those places. Happiness, joy, and contentment are not found in a geographical location. They are found in Christ!

We should be content with whatever God gives us. Hebrews 13:5 reminds us, "Let your conversation be without covetousness; and be content with such things as ye have: for he hath said, I will never leave thee, nor forsake thee." First Timothy 6:8 says, "And having food and raiment let us be therewith content." Luke 12:15 says, "And he said unto them, Take heed, and beware of covetousness: for a man's life consisteth not in the abundance of the things which he possesseth." These and many other verses in the Bible teach us that things cannot bring happiness, joy, and contentment. Contentment is not found in possessions. It is found in Christ!

We should be content with those whom God places around us. We often blame our lack of contentment on the people with whom we work. You have heard the saying, "It is hard to soar with the eagles when you have to work with the buzzards." Whether or not we like it, God has a purpose for everyone He places in our lives. Some are a great blessing to us. Others seem like holy sandpaper. But we need both! Contentment is not found in another person. It is found in the God-man, Jesus Christ.

STAY IN LOVE

The great love chapter emphasizes the absolute necessity of love. First Corinthians 13:1–3 says, "Though I speak with the tongues of men and of angels, and have not charity, I am become as sounding brass, or a tinkling cymbal. And though I have the gift of prophecy, and understand all mysteries, and all knowledge; and though I have all faith, so that I could remove mountains, and have not charity, I am nothing. And though I bestow all my goods to feed the poor, and though I give my body to be burned, and have not charity, it profiteth me nothing."

Love is more important than eloquence. Love exceeds the gift of interpreting prophecy. Love is more powerful than faith. Love is above benevolence. Love is even greater than martyrdom. The bottom line is that all of these things, without love, are worthless. Love is the indispensable ingredient in the Christian's ministry.

Stay in love with the Lord. Don't ever let your love for Him grow cold. When you feel yourself drifting from Him, do whatever it takes to rekindle that love. Sing hymns and praises to Him. Express your love to Him. Show Him that you love Him by your actions. I often wonder if the Lord does not whisper to us as he did to Peter, "Lovest thou me more than these?" (John 21:15).

Stay in love with your mate. We have to work at loving our mates, just as we work at other things. We should be as kind to our mates after the wedding as we were when we were trying to convince them to be our mates. Recently I was sitting by a young Christian on a plane trip from California to Atlanta. He asked how long I had been married. He was contemplating marriage, but was somewhat fearful because he had seen some failed marriages. I told him that I had been married for fifty-eight years and that I was still working at our marriage. He seemed shocked that after that long you would still need to work at marriage. I explained to him that working at marriage was necessary because I was married to a woman. Of course, Virginia could say she has to work at it because she is married to a man. Whatever it takes, a lasting, loving marriage is worth the effort!

Stay in love with your children. Your children are a heritage from the Lord. They are precious gifts. We should never get so busy in our work that we neglect our children. More than they need the things you provide or give, they need you. We have our children in our homes for such a short time. Express your love to them. Be ready to commend them for the good things they do. Love them enough to discipline them. Love them in spite of their mistakes. Stay in love with them.

Love is the indispensable ingredient in the Christian's ministry.

They will produce your grandchildren, and no grandparent needs to be encouraged to love their grandchildren.

Stay in love with your God-given ministry. Love what God has committed into your hand. Treasure it. Listen to the testimony of the Apostle Paul after he had been in the ministry most of his life: "And I thank Christ Jesus our Lord, who hath enabled me, for that he counted me faithful, putting me into the ministry" (1 Timothy 1:12). Paul's life had not been easy. He suffered as only few people have ever suffered. He was persecuted. He was scourged five times. He was stoned. He was beaten. He was imprisoned. But at the end of his life, he thanked God that he had been blessed to be in the ministry.

Stay Pure

If you are to finish well you must stay pure. First Timothy 5:1–2 teaches, "Rebuke not an elder, but intreat him as a father; and the younger men as brethren; The elder women as mothers; the younger as sisters, with all purity." Great advice, is it not? Our relationships with older men should be as to a father. Our relationships with older ladies should be as to a mother. Our relationships with the younger men should be as to a brother. And our relationships with younger ladies should be as to a sister in all purity.

Purity is absolutely necessary if we are to finish well. If we are to be effective in the fourth quarter, we must stay pure.

Be pure in your thinking. This is where all impurity begins. "Guard your heart" is the advice of the wise man. I have never dealt with a case of immorality that did not begin with pornography. Just don't go there. Never, never, never start viewing the wrong things. It will control your thinking, and your thinking will control your actions.

Be pure in your speech. Don't allow yourself to indulge in questionable jokes or stories. Don't listen to them. Refuse to participate in innuendo and inappropriate talk. On more than a few occasions, I have had to let even believers know that I did not want to hear a joke or any speech that was not pure.

Be pure in your actions. Most immoral relationships begin with what one would describe as innocent flirtations. By the way, they are not innocent! We must be discreet in our actions in relationships with the opposite sex. The mind is a strange organ. When little thoughts enter the mind, they become enlarged. It is like the story of the camel getting his nose in the tent. Once the nose is there, the camel will eventually take over the entire tent.

James gives us a very clear picture of how something small can be the beginning of our destruction. James 1:14–16 says, "But every man is tempted, when he is drawn away of his own lust, and enticed. Then when lust hath conceived, it bringeth forth sin: and sin, when it is finished, bringeth forth death. Do not err, my beloved brethren."

There is no bargain basement sale for sin. The price is always the same. Death to your purity, death to your marriage, death to your innocence, death to your family, and death to your self respect—these are just a few of the results of yielding to temptations, regardless of how small they appear.

To finish your course with joy, you must choose to be content, to stay in love, and to stay pure. Let's move on to one more principle that will help you stay faithful until death.

TEN

All for the Glory of God

What is the purpose of man? Why are we permitted to occupy this earth for a period of time?

A great way to begin every day is to stop and recognize that every day is a gift from God. I begin each day by thanking God for the day and asking for His guidance and His grace. We need both—guidance and grace. We need His guidance step by step. We also need His grace to face the challenges and trials that come our way.

The Apostle Paul shows us the purpose for man in 1 Corinthians 10:31: "Whether therefore ye eat, or drink, or whatsoever ye do, do all to the glory of God." If I desire to finish well, I must keep my ultimate purpose in mind. Over the centuries, many have quoted the statement, "Man's chief end is to glorify God and to enjoy Him for eternity." Let's consider this statement more closely.

In a lesson that I teach entitled, "How to Stay in the Ministry All Your Life," my last point states, "Spend your time glorifying God, not promoting yourself." Jesus taught His disciples that this was His purpose for us. In Matthew 5:14–16 He said, "Ye are the light of the world. A city that is set on an hill cannot be hid, Neither do men light a candle, and put it under a bushel, but on a candlestick; and it giveth light unto all that are in the house. Let your light so shine before men, that they may see your good works, and glorify your Father which is in heaven."

Self-promotion is very popular, but not spiritually prosperous.

Notice it is not that they may see your good works and glorify *you*. It is not that they may glorify your denomination, your Bible college, or even your family. God has told us plainly that He will not share His glory. In Isaiah 48:11 He says, "For mine own sake, even for mine own sake, will I do it: for how should my name be polluted? And I will not give my glory unto another." Self-promotion is very popular, but not spiritually prosperous.

It is sad to say, but many ministries are so consumed with receiving glory that they miss the primary purpose of ministry. We must learn to defer all glory to Him!

First Chronicles 16:29 reminds us, "Give unto the LORD the glory due unto his name." Whatever glory is put upon us must readily be given to the Lord. By the grace of God we are what we are.

Regardless of our age, our circumstances, or any other factor, we are to glorify our great God.

How can we best glorify God? Let me share four ways you can glorify God in your fourth quarter.

WHEN I HAVE A GENUINE APPRECIATION FOR GOD, I GLORIFY HIM

I think often of the passage in Psalm 37. In verse 23 David makes this statement—"The steps of a good man are ordered by the LORD: and he delighteth in his way." Two things come to my mind. One is that the Lord delights in the way of the good man. The good man is not a super-saint. There is no such creature. He is merely a man who has the imputed righteousness of the Lord Jesus Christ. When we trust Jesus, His righteousness is placed upon us. Second Corinthians 5:21 says, "For he hath made him to be sin for us, who knew no sin; that we might be made the righteousness of God in him." When God looks at the good man, He is pleased.

The second thought is that the good man delights in the Lord. How often do you stop and consider how good God is? By the way, He is always good. When we are pleased with God in all circumstances, He is glorified in our lives. One preacher has rightly said, "God is most glorified in us when we are most satisfied in Him." When God is glorified, God's people should be satisfied. Psalm 97:9 says, "For thou, LORD, art high above all the earth: thou art exalted far above all gods." This should be our continual thinking about Him.

WHEN I PRAISE HIM, I GLORIFY HIM

Psalm 29:2 says, "Give unto the LORD the glory due unto his name; worship the LORD in the beauty of holiness." Psalm 149:1, "Praise ye the LORD. Sing unto the LORD a new song, and his praise in the congregation of saints."

Psalm 150:1–6, "Praise ye the LORD. Praise God in his sanctuary: praise him in the firmament of his power. Praise him for his mighty acts: praise him according to his excellent greatness. Praise him with the sound of the trumpet: praise him with the psaltery and harp. Praise him with the timbrel and dance: praise him with stringed instruments and organs. Praise him upon the loud cymbals: praise him upon the high sounding cymbals. Let every thing that hath breath praise the LORD. Praise ye the LORD."

From these and many other Bible passages, we understand that God desires to be praised. We glorify Him by our praise. As I write these words, we are just a few days away from Resurrection Sunday. I think of the great crowds who praised the Lord as He was riding a donkey into Jerusalem. Luke 19:37–38 tells us, "And when he was come nigh, even now at the descent of the mount of Olives, the whole multitude of the disciples began to rejoice and praise God with a loud voice for all the mighty works that they had seen; Saying, Blessed be the King that cometh in the name of the Lord: peace in heaven, and glory in the highest."

God was glorified by the crowd's praise. When the Pharisees criticized these praising people, the Lord justified their praise by saying, "If these should hold their peace, the stones would immediately cry out" (Luke 19:40). I think He was saying, "I desire to be praised. In fact, I *will* be praised!" Every time I read these words I think, "I do not want the stones to do my praising." Every day we can find so many things for which to praise God. When we praise Him, we are blessed and He is glorified.

WHEN I LOVE HIM, I GLORIFY HIM

Deuteronomy 6:4–5 says, "Hear, O Israel: The LORD our God is one LORD: And thou shalt love the LORD thy God with all thine heart, and with all thy soul, and with all thy might." When asked concerning the greatest commandment, Jesus replied in Matthew 22:37, "Thou shalt love the Lord thy God with all thy heart, and with all thy soul, and with all thy mind."

Some of the sweetest words our ears can hear are, "I love you." Those are pleasing words to a young man when they come from a girl he is pursuing. They are sweet words to a mother when they come from a son or daughter. They are sweet words when they are uttered from the lips and the heart of a mate. We may already know that the person loves us, but we never tire of hearing it spoken.

Our great God knows all about us. He knows more about us than we know about ourselves. But He desires to hear those words from His children. We should say them to Him often and they should come from our hearts, not just our lips. When was the last time you told the Lord you love Him? Why not do it now?

Three times, Peter denied the Lord. After the Resurrection, Peter decided to go back to his old occupation. In John 21:2–3 we read, "There were together Simon Peter, and Thomas called Didymus, and Nathanael of Cana in Galilee, and the sons of Zebedee, and two other of his disciples. Simon Peter saith unto them, I go a fishing. They say unto him, We also go with thee."

Have you not noticed that no one gets out of the will of God alone? They always influence others to do the same. Influence is a trust, and we must use it wisely. In the latter part of the chapter, Jesus is in the process of restoring Peter to his purpose for his life. Three times he asks the simple question, "Lovest thou me?" God desires the love of His people.

One of the qualifications for discipleship is supreme love. Luke 14:26 says, "If any man come to me, and hate not his father, and mother, and wife, and children, and brethren, and sisters, yea, and his own life also, he cannot be my disciple." In this verse, Jesus is not encouraging us to hate our parents, our wife, or our children. He is saying that in comparison to our love for Him, all other love should fade into insignificance.

When was the last time you told the Lord you love Him?

I shall never forget the words of a young man going through great persecution because of his faith in Christ. His family had signified that he did not love his siblings, his parents, or his country. I heard him pour out his heart to God. "Lord, you know that I love my parents. You know that I love my siblings. You know that I love my country. But Lord, I love you more than all of these." What a great example of supreme love. That was forty-five years ago, and God has richly honored that love.

The fact that we are getting older should not be a reason for our love for the Lord to lessen.

WHEN I OBEY HIM, I GLORIFY HIM

Luke 6:46 says, "And why call ye me, Lord, Lord, and do not the things which I say?" In this verse, Jesus is rebuking his followers for empty words. They were calling Him "Lord," but they were not doing what He had commanded them to do. I like the saying, "When all is said and done, there is a lot more said than done."

When I obey the Lord, I am saying that I believe everything He says to me, and that I am willing to act on that belief.

See what David said to Saul when the army of Israel was being threatened by Goliath: "And David said to Saul, Let no man's heart fail because of him; thy servant will go and fight with this Philistine" (1 Samuel 17:32). When we know what God desires for us to do, our resolve should be, "I will do it regardless of the consequences." The best way to find out what God wants us to do is to read the Bible. When we read His Word and do what is written in it, He is glorified. We often refer to ourselves as Bible-believing Christians, but do we really believe it? Belief that does not affect our behavior is a false belief.

Do you, like the Apostle Paul, have a burning desire and determination to finish your course with joy? Then don't just sit in the rocking chair, expecting to be pampered, merely entertaining yourself. Like Caleb, dare to claim all that God has for you in your fourth quarter.

CONCLUSION
Finishing Your Course with Joy

I think of how blessed we are in the United States of America. Older people are respected in many countries around the world. However, not many countries afford the opportunities for our age group as does our country.

For instance, when I visit McDonald's, I am able to get "senior coffee." (Most of my friends think that I get my coffee from McDonald's because I am cheap. I am, but primarily, I just really like their coffee.) When I visit a golf course, I can often receive a reduced green fee. The same is true when I check into a motel room. In fact, just about everything I do, I get a discount just because of my age. I am not opposed to this. In fact, I really like it. I do have to admit that I feel rather badly when a young family comes to the same place and pays a higher price for the same service. I often think, "They are the ones that should get the discount!"

Most people in their later years are able to draw social security. Years ago, I really did not think I would receive a benefit from social security, but I got old faster than I realized I would! Most people over sixty have had their homes long enough to pay them off. Many senior citizens have several other benefits such as Medicare or discounted drug programs. I mention this only to say that we are in a position to contribute more generously to the cause of Christ through our churches. This is one of the ways that we can be greatly used during the "fourth quarter" of our lives.

Some studies indicate that 60 percent of the wealth of our country will change hands in the next twenty years. I wonder if we have placed our churches and other Christian ministries in our wills and trust funds? I often hear of an estate being left to the most ridiculous cause, and I think of the many Christian ministries that could have been greatly helped by that money.

Since retirement frees us from the customary forty-hour workweek, we have time that the younger generation can only dream of. By the way, most of them will have to work much longer to reach the position than we have obtained. (If you haven't retired yet, I'm sorry about that bit of bad news.)

I am not suggesting that we deprive ourselves of this well-deserved, more leisurely lifestyle. I am, however, suggesting that we do not get so comfortable in our rocking chairs and so involved in our hobbies and other forms of entertainment that we forget that God still has a purpose for us in His work.

I often hear the statement, "I would rather burn out than rust out." Every time I hear this, I think, "Are these the only two options?" I don't like either one! I don't think we are limited to those two options. We still have the option to finish strong for the glory of God.

I would suggest that you pre-determine your course. Make some commitments to certain activities in which you would really like to be involved. If I wake up every day with no agenda or direction, I am going to waste a lot of time just determining what to do with my day. It is far better to have a pre-set schedule to follow. For certain, that planned scheduled will be interrupted quite often, but without it, we wouldn't even get started.

By the same token, you are at liberty to change your schedule. You are a volunteer. You have privileges. For instance, rather than a two-week vacation, you could schedule a one-week vacation each month. Rather than having a day off each week, you may choose to have two days off each week. Rather than working from eight to five you may choose to work from ten to two. You can choose your hours and your days. Whatever time you give to the organization or local church will benefit the Lord's work.

You should also schedule time for inactivity and for recreation. It would be good for most of us to schedule some extended time for our children and grandchildren, if they have time for us. You have earned it. God has blessed your faithfulness to your work. Now He will bless you as you seek to be a blessing to others.

I have some time scheduled to be in northern Illinois around the end of May. A little boy, Nathanael, is expected to be born around that time. He will be our first great-grandchild. Aren't we glad to have these liberties? I have another week carved out this summer for a preacher's golf tournament. My handicap will be so high, I may just be able to win!

As I finish this little book, the annual NBA playoffs are under way. In reality there is no need to watch the entire game—I am too involved with my "retirement activities" to do that. I have, however, been able to see the final minutes of several of the games. The result of the entire game is nearly always determined by the play in the final minutes. I have no idea who will be the NBA champs this year. (I don't really care.) But I know that whoever wins will have to do well in the fourth quarter. The fourth quarter is vital.

So it is in the game of life! The fourth quarter is always vital. Don't blow it. Finish strong!

I am so thrilled that I did not become inactive in the work of God during my fourth quarter. I think of all that I would have missed. I would have missed the opportunity to have met and served with some of the greatest people on the earth. I would not have been able lead many of the people to the Lord that I have in the last ten years. (The Saturday before Easter, my soulwinning partner and I saw two precious people trust Jesus Christ as their Saviour.)

I would not have had the opportunity to be involved with hundreds of young people who are training for the ministry. I would not have been able to see over fifty million dollars committed to missions in the past ten years.

My golf handicap may have been lower. I may have been able to visit some places and do some things that I would have enjoyed. I may have had a lot more leisure time. However, I would not think about trading the things I have gained for the things that I missed. I didn't miss anything that will matter in eternity.

Lest you think it has all been a sacrifice in the last ten years, let me mention a few things we have been blessed with simply by being where God led us.

In September of 2006, we learned that my wife, Virginia, had a large tumor at the base of her brain. In our church was a lady who was employed at one of the largest medical facilities in the world. Shelly Cole was able to refer my wife to one of the foremost neurosurgeons in the world. The result of the operation was 100 percent successful.

Virginia and I were also privileged to be involved in a cruise to Alaska. We have been privileged to go to many great places and do many things that we only dreamed about when we were young. I have had the opportunity to, without any expense to myself, play some of the greatest golf courses in the world. (To mention just a few—Pebble Beach, Torrey Pines, King and Bear, Slammer and Squire, and the five championship courses at Desert Hot Springs, La Quinta resort. I am still waiting for someone to get me on at Augusta National. I am "retired," so I can make time in my schedule.)

Hey, gang (my crowd over sixty), this is our time! By God's grace, let's show those coming behind us how to finish well. Let's leave a legacy for others that shows them how to finish their course with joy for the glory of God!

As we close, consider this paragraph from Sherwood Eliot Wirt's book *I Don't Know What Old Is:*

> Bumper stickers keep informing us that "happiness is being a grandparent." Grandchildren are certainly a blessing; in our house their affection always gives us a lift. Real inner joy, however, does not stem from

dependence on relationships with other individuals, not even grandchildren. It comes from a vision of what life is for and the translation of that vision into reality. It does not derive from Social Security or Medicare, great as these helps are to retirement. It derives from an acknowledgment that the Creator of the universe is our Heavenly Father, that Jesus Christ is His Son, and that we belong to Him forever.

Play well the first three quarters, but whatever you do, have a great fourth quarter!

Accomplishments During Fourth Quarters

At age 58

- Sony Chairman Akio Morita introduced the Sony Walkman, even though nobody seemed to like the idea prior to its release.

- President Thomas Jefferson introduced the custom of having White House guests shake hands instead of bowing stiffly.

- Jacob Perkins created a compression machine, paving the way for the invention of gas refrigeration.

At age 59

- Einstein achieved a major new result in the general theory of relativity.

- English novelist and journalist Daniel Defoe wrote his first and most famous novel, *The Life and Adventures of Robinson Crusoe*.
- "Satchel" Paige became the oldest Major League baseball player.
- Clara Barton founded the American Red Cross.
- Cellist Nancy Donaruma retired from the New York Philharmonic to become a full-time paramedic.
- After nine years of sacrificing in the United States, Ana Torres hired a shrimp boat and rode on it to get her sons out of Cuba during the Mariel boatlift.

At age 65

- Self-taught American primitive artist, Morris Hirshfield, began painting.
- Kathe Smith of south Georgia was raising her two-year-old grandson, while taking care of the house, yard, swimming pool, five dogs and three cats, walking two miles a day pushing said grandson in a stroller, and exercising regularly with cats and grandson crawling all over her. This was done despite having nerve damage on the left side of her body and being "disabled" for twelve years.

At age 66

- Noah Webster completed his monumental *American Dictionary of the English Language*.

- The composer, Franck, wrote his only symphony.
- American physician, Francis Townsend, paved the way for Social Security by suggesting that all retirees over the age of sixty should receive $200 a month.

At age 69

- English writer and lexicographer Samuel Johnson began his last major work, *The Lives of the English Poets*.
- James Hutton originated the modern theory of the formation of the earth's crust.
- Ronald Wilson Reagan became the oldest man ever sworn in as President of the United States. He was sworn in again four years later.
- Werner Berger became the oldest North American to scale the highest peaks on each of the world's seven continents. He proposed to his girlfriend before he left.

At age 70

- Benjamin Franklin helped draft the Declaration of Independence.
- Businessman Cornelius Vanderbilt began buying railroads.
- Justice John W. Sirica heard the Watergate case.
- Judy Brenner, who had recently run the Boston Marathon, chased a teenage shoplifter one hundred feet and helped hold him until police arrived.

At age 71

- Einstein proposed a new version of the unified field theory, but other physicists considered it untenable.
- Casey Stengel began managing the New York Mets.
- Bill Horning won first place in his division in the 2004 U.S. Adult National Figure Skating Championships.
- Katsusuke Yanagisawa, a retired Japanese schoolteacher, became the oldest person to climb Mount Everest.

At age 72

- Margaret Ringenberg flew around the world.
- Retired mining engineer Ed Whitlock became the first man over seventy to run a standard marathon in under three hours (2:59:10). (The best marathon of his career was 2:31:23 at age forty-eight.)
- Harry Truman received an honorary Civic Law degree from Oxford University.

At age 74

- Ferdinand Marie de Lesseps began an attempt to construct the Suez Canal.
- Tom Morris, Sr. was possibly the oldest professional golfer.
- A Maori woman, Ramari Port, received her Ph.D. in molecular medicine from the University of Auckland.

- Chuck Yeager reenacted his first breaking of the sound barrier fifty years earlier.
- Thomas Selfridge went to Afghanistan as a consultant to help rebuild the highway from Kabul to Qandahar.

At age 77

- Grandma Moses started painting.
- John Glenn became the oldest person to go into space in a study of how space flight affects the elderly.
- Helen Heubi obtained her Ph.D. in Therapeutic Counseling. She had to fit in two cataract operations while doing the last-minute work.

At age 78

- Emma Hanner made an emergency landing in a field west of St. Louis after the propeller on her two-seater plane suddenly stopped. This was her first emergency landing in nearly four decades of flying.
- Justice Oliver Wendell Holmes, Jr. gave his definition of the limits to free speech. He said the First Amendment would not protect someone "falsely shouting 'fire' in a theatre and causing a panic."

At age 79

- Asa A. Long became the oldest United States checkers champion.

- Actor Jimmy Stewart worked to enhance public appreciation and understanding of the Constitution and Bill of Rights.
- John Powanda became the oldest Peace Corps volunteer in history.

At age 80

- American writer and physician Oliver Wendell Holmes published *Over the Teacups*, which displayed his characteristic vitality and wit.
- Christine Brown of Laguna Hills, California, flew to China and climbed the Great Wall.

At age 81

- After thirty-seven years out of the cockpit, daredevil pilot Mary Victor Bruce flew a loop-the-loop.
- Cincinnati resident, Harold Berkshire, graduated from high school.
- Bill Painter became the oldest person to reach the 14,411-foot summit of Mount Rainier.
- Barbara McClintock won the Nobel Prize in "Physiology or Medicine" for the discovery of genetic transposition.
- Rosa Parks received the Rosa Parks Peace Prize in Stockholm, Sweden.

At age 82

- The renowned writer, Johann Wolfgang von Goethe, finished writing *Faust*, with which he had begun experimenting more than sixty years earlier.
- William Ivy Baldwin became the oldest tightrope walker, crossing the South Boulder Canyon in Colorado on a 320-foot wire.
- Winston Churchill wrote *A History of the English-Speaking Peoples*.
- Leo Tolstoy wrote *I Cannot Be Silent*.
- Rita Roherty hit ninety-one of one hundred clay pigeons to take third place in a rifle competition.
- Venus Ramey balanced on her walker and fired her handgun to shoot out an intruder's tires. Ramey, winner of the 1944 Miss America pageant, confronted an intruder on her Kentucky farm and disabled his vehicle so he couldn't escape.

At age 83

- Great grandmother Joyce Patrick learned to read and write.

At age 85

- American businessman, inventor, and philanthropist, Peter Cooper, ran for president as nominee of the Greenback party.
- "Coco" Chanel was the head of a fashion design firm.

- Theodor Mommsen became the oldest person to receive a Nobel Prize in Literature.

At age 86
- Katherine Pelton swam the two hundred meter butterfly in 3 minutes, 1.14 seconds, beating the men's world record for the 85 to 89 age group by over twenty seconds.

At age 88
- Michelangelo created the architectural plans for the Church of Santa Maria degli Angeli.
- Claude Pepper was the oldest man ever elected to the United States House of Representatives.
- Walter Hart became an Eagle Scout, the highest rank in the Boy Scouts. He finished the requirements seventy years earlier, but never received the award because he joined the Navy during World War II.

At age 89
- Artur Rubinstein performed one of his greatest recitals in Carnegie Hall.
- Albert Schweitzer ran a hospital in Africa.

At age 91
- Hulda Crooks climbed Mt. Whitney.

- Allan Stewart of New South Wales completed a Bachelor of Laws degree from the University of New England. He finished what would have normally been a six-year degree in four and a half years.

At age 93

- Theodore Francis Green retired from the U.S. Senate. At that time, he was the oldest senator in the history of the institution.
- Strom Thurmond, the longest-serving senator in U.S. history, won reelection after promising not to run again at age 99.
- George Bernard Shaw wrote the play "Farfetched Fables."
- P.G. Wodehouse worked on his ninety-seventh novel and was knighted the same year.

At age 96

- The art designer Erte, promising never to retire, worked on sets and costumes for two Manhattan musicals, and worked on remodeling his estate on Majorca, planting fruit trees to be enjoyed in his old age.
- Harry Bernstein published his first book *The Invisible Wall*, which recounted his childhood in an English mill town. He started writing it at ninety-three as a way to deal with the loss of his wife of almost seventy years.

- Dorothy Geeben was the mayor of Ocean Breeze Park, Florida, and may have been the oldest mayor in the United States.

At age 99
- Harold Mark Foster of Owensboro, Kentucky, began learning to read.
- Teiichi Igarashi climbed Mount Fuji.
- Twice in one year, Kathleen Slater successfully fought off intruders who attacked her in the middle of the night.

At age 100+
- Alice Porlock of Great Britain published her first book, *Portrait of My Victorian Youth*, when she was 102 years old.
- Jeanne Calment, 122, was recognized as the world's oldest living person.
- The biblical patriarch, Methuselah, died at the age of 969.

Visit us online

strivingtogether.com

wcbc.edu

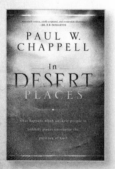

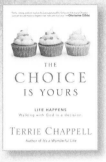
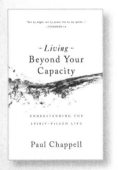

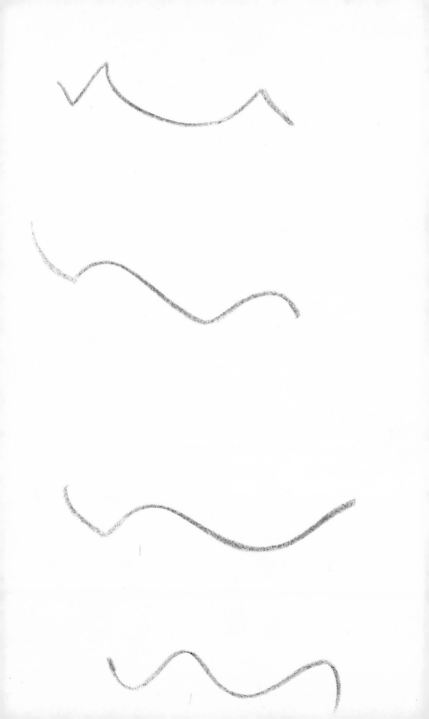